World in Focus
Germany

HODDER
Wayland

DAVID FLINT

First published in 2005 by Hodder Wayland,
an imprint of Hodder Children's Books
© Hodder Wayland 2005

Commissioning editor: Victoria Brooker
Editor: Patience Coster
Inside design: Chris Halls, www.mindseyedesign.co.uk
Cover design: Hodder Wayland
 Series concept and project management by EASI-Educational Resourcing
(info@easi-er.co.uk)
Statistical research: Anna Bowden
Maps and graphs: Martin Darlison, Encompass Graphics

British Library Cataloguing in Publication Data

Flint, David, 1946-
   Germany. - (World in focus)
   1. Germany - Juvenile literature
   I. Title
   943'.0882

ISBN: 0750246847

Printed and bound in China

Hodder Children's Books
A division of Hodder Headline Limited
338 Euston Road, London NW1 3BH

Cover top: A busy street in Heidelberg.
Cover bottom: Main square in Griefswald.
Title page: Young people enjoy May Day in Bavaria.

Picture acknowledgements.The author and publisher would like to thank the following for
allowing their pictures to be reproduced in this publication:
Corbis 8 (Archivo Iconografico, S. A.), 21 (Alex Grimm/Reuters), 22 (Brooks Kraft), 24 (Owen Franken), 34
(Reuters), 37 (Reuters), 44 (Fabrizio Bensch), 52 (Ken Straiton), 56 (Bossu Regis); EASI-Images/Edward
Parker *cover top and bottom,* 4, 5, 6, 9, 10, 11, 12, 13, 14, 15, 16, 17, 18, 19, 20, 23, 25, 26, 27, 28, 29, 30, 31, 32,
33, 35, 36, 38, 39, 40, 41, 42, 43, 45, 46 and *title page*, 47, 48, 49, 50, 51, 53, 54, 55, 57, 58 and 59.

The website addresses (URLs) included in this book were valid at the time of going to press.
However, because of the nature of the Internet, it is possible that some addresses may have
changed, or sites may have changed or closed down since publication. While the author and
Publishers regret any inconvenience this may cause the readers, no responsibility for any such
changes can be accepted by either the author or the Publisher.

The directional arrow portrayed on the map on page 7 provides only an approximation of north.
The data used to produce the graphics and data panels in this title were the latest available at the
time of production.

CONTENTS

CHAPTER 1

Germany – An Overview

Germany is a large, economically powerful and important country at the heart of Europe. It has close links with its neighbours and is a leading member of the European Union (EU), a joining together of 25 countries that was founded in 1958. Germany extends around 800 km (497 miles) from the Baltic coast and North Sea in the north to the borders of Austria and Switzerland in the south. It extends about 700 km (435 miles) from the French, Belgian and Dutch borders in the west to the Polish and Czech borders in the east. It covers a total area of 357,021 sq km (137,846 sq miles), which makes it slightly smaller than the US state of Montana.

GERMANY'S DEVELOPMENT AS A NATION

As a result of its history, culture and politics, Germany has had a greater impact on Europe than any other country on the continent. In the nineteenth century, Germany was unified under Otto von Bismarck, the leader of the state of Prussia. Bismarck successfully waged war against Denmark in 1864 and against Austria in 1866 to create a North German federation. In 1871 he added South Germany to

▼ The refurbished Olympic stadium in the foreground of this photo of Berlin confirms the continued growth and importance of Germany's capital city.

this region to create what is now known as modern Germany. During the nineteenth century, this area enjoyed great economic success because of its natural resources of coal, iron and lignite which were used to develop heavy industries such as steel-making, chemicals and engineering.

During the twentieth century, Germany fought and lost two world wars (see pages 10-11), and was divided into two separate states (East and West Germany). In 1990 the country was re-united again as one nation. Today integration is proceeding rapidly, but there are still important differences between the eastern and western parts of the country. In the former eastern region, for example, there are huge co-operative farms, while in the former western region there are smaller, traditional farms.

INDUSTRY AND THE ECONOMY

During the twentieth century, the German economy grew rapidly. This was the result of government directives that managed to harness the country's rich resources. The German economy is now so large and powerful that it is central to the development of Europe as a whole. Germany has brought about some of the most advanced and innovative industrial developments ever. German manufactured goods, such as cars and

▲ Southern Germany, particularly the state of Bavaria, has countryside dotted with farms and small villages separated by areas of dense forest.

electronics equipment, are sold all over the world and Germany is a major world importer of goods such as timber and textiles.

MOUNTAINS, CASTLES AND CITIES

Germany is famous for its beautiful landscapes, from the mountains of Bavaria in the south to the sand dunes of the Baltic coast in the north. There are fabulous mystical castles, often perched on top of impossibly steep hillsides above rivers such as the Rhine and the Elbe. There are historic small villages and beautiful stretches of countryside, especially in the Black Forest area in the south. German cities are vibrant, multicultural and progressive. They are evolving rapidly, especially in the case of the capital, Berlin, with its numerous new buildings. There are also many great German museums and architectural gems, the result of 2,000 years of history.

REMARKABLE GERMANS

Culturally, Germany has produced a wealth of extraordinarily talented people, including the musical composers Johann Sebastian Bach and Ludwig von Beethoven, the writers Johann Wolfgang von Goethe and Fredrich von Schiller, the scientist Albert Einstein, the philosophers Martin Heidegger and Emmanuel Kant, and the political writer Karl Marx.

Physical geography

- Land area: 349,223 sq km/134,835 sq miles
- Water area: 7,798 sq km/3,011 sq miles
- Total area: 357,021 sq km/137,846 sq miles
- World rank (by area): 62
- Land boundaries:3,621 km/2,249 miles
- Border countries: Austria, Belgium, Czech Republic, Denmark, France, Luxembourg, Netherlands, Poland, Switzerland
- Coastline: 2,389 km/1,484 miles
- Highest point: Zugspitze (2,963 m/9,721 ft)
- Lowest point: Neuendorf bei Wilster (-3.54 m/-11.6 ft)

Source: CIA World Factbook

◄ With its narrow streets and baroque churches and buildings, Heidelberg is typical of the older German cities.

CHAPTER 2

History

The earliest inhabitants of Germany were Celts. In the fourth century BC, the Celts were gradually displaced by fair-haired Scandinavian tribes from the north and west and Slav tribes from the east.

THE HOLY ROMAN EMPIRE

In 58 BC, the Romans occupied the western banks of the Rhine. In AD 436, tribes led by Attila the Hun (King of the Huns, lived c.406–453) helped to defeat the Romans. Germany was subsequently divided up and ruled by tribal leaders. In the eighth century, the king of the Franks, Charlemagne (lived c.742–814), united by force much of what is present-day France and Germany. On Charlemagne's death, his empire was broken up. In 962, the eastern part of this old empire became the Holy Roman Empire, which lasted until 1806. The Holy Roman Empire was a loose assembly of states. It gained its name because, from Charlemagne onwards, the kings of this territory protected the Christian authority of the Pope in Rome.

THE REFORMATION

In the sixteenth century, a professor of theology named Martin Luther objected to the selling of indulgences (buying freedom from punishment for a sin) by the Roman Catholic Church. His objections sparked the Reformation, a movement to reform the Roman Catholic Church, and the

Did you know?

In AD 786, Charlemagne defeated the armies of Lombardy and became the protector of the papal state in Rome. He was crowned kaiser (king) in AD 800 by a grateful Pope, whose armies had been on the point of defeat.

◀ This is a detail of the shrine of Charlemagne, which is situated in the Palatine Chapel in the German city of Aachen.

 Bavarian Protestants attending church. On public occasions, many German people wear traditional costume to show their strong links to the local area.

growth of a new Protestant Church. The Reformation led to a split within the states of the Holy Roman Empire. By 1555, it was up to the prince of each state in the area that is now Germany to choose which would be his province's main religion.

THE THIRTY YEARS' WAR

From 1618 to 1648, the Holy Roman Empire was ravaged by the Thirty Years' War. Protestant and Catholic states fought with one another over their religious differences. The conflict was so long and bloody that, by 1648 when the war ended, Germany was devastated. The Empire took a hundred years to recover from the effects of the Thirty Years' War and many of the smaller states struggled to survive. Larger states, such as Prussia managed to grow and develop, but this process was overtaken by

the invasion of the French. In 1806, the French emperor, Napoléon Bonaparte, defeated local armies and ended the Holy Roman Empire. In 1815, following Napoléon's defeat by a coalition of British, Russian and Prussian armies, Germany was reorganized into a confederation of 35 states, all of which were fiercely independent.

? Did you know?

Between 1348 and 1350, the Black Death (bubonic plague) killed one in every four people in Germany.

BISMARCK

In the 1830s the Industrial Revolution came to Germany: mines were excavated, steel and engineering works opened and new railway lines built. With its military might and its plentiful natural resources, Prussia became one of the strongest states in the German Confederation. In 1871, Otto von Bismarck emerged as Prussia's chancellor, keen to unite Germany under Prussian rule.

By skilful diplomacy, Bismarck finally managed to unite Germany in 1871, with Berlin as its capital. The national colours were established as black, red and white (later gold). Germany began a process of rapid industrialization. By 1890, Germany had established important coal, steel, engineering, electrical and chemicals industries. She also began to build up a powerful army and navy.

FIRST WORLD WAR

In 1914, the assassination of Franz Ferdinand, Archduke of Austria, in Sarajevo, triggered the start of the First World War. The war saw an alliance of Germany, Austria and Turkey (the Central Powers) against Britain, France and Russia (the Allied Powers). In 1917, the USA entered the war on the side of the Allies, who triumphed over the Central Powers in 1918. Following her defeat in the First World War, Germany was politically and economically weak. This situation contributed to the growth of extremist groups like the Nazi Party.

▼ This is part of the original stadium built by the Nazis in Berlin for the 1936 Olympic games. At the games, Hitler and his supporters tried, and failed, to convince the world of the supremacy of their ideas.

THE NAZI ERA

During the 1930s, German nationalism also became a major force in uniting the country and leading to the rise of the Nazis. In 1933, Adolf Hitler came to power. His Nazi Party was popular with the German people because it brought about economic success. It did this by investing heavily in employment programmes, such as building new motorways (*autobahnen*). It also encouraged the rapid growth of industries, especially shipbuilding, chemicals and aircraft manufacture and others linked with the armed forces. The Nazis believed in a superior 'Aryan' race of pure Germans. They blamed the Jews and other minority groups for Germany's economic and social problems, and organized boycotts of Jewish businesses and expelled Jews from jobs in teaching, medicine and other public services.

By 1939, Germany was prosperous and powerful and had rebuilt her armed forces. Hitler saw his chance to expand German territory for Aryan occupation. In September 1939, the Nazis invaded Poland and, as a result, Britain and France declared war on Germany. In 1941, the USA and the Soviet Union joined forces with Britain and France. These allies defeated Germany in 1945. During the war, the Nazis had begun a systematic attempt to kill all Jews in the parts of Europe they conquered. They set up concentration camps, many of which provided slave labour for large factories. Most of these camps were in Eastern Europe, and some of them had gas chambers where it is estimated that six million Jews were murdered during what is known as 'The Holocaust'. After the war, British, US, French and Soviet troops occupied Germany.

 Did you know?

On 13 February 1945, British aircraft bombed and destroyed most of the ancient German city of Dresden. Parts of the city were later rebuilt according to the old pattern.

Focus on: Concentration camps

During the Second World War, the Nazis used concentration camps to detain and kill millions of Jews, political opponents, homosexuals, gypsies, disabled people and resistance fighters. There were 22 concentration camps under Nazi control. In camps such as Auschwitz, Belsen, Sobibor and Treblinka, inmates were gassed, shot, beaten or tortured to death. Seven million people were sent to concentration camps, but only 500,000 people survived. Today many of these camps have been preserved and are open to the public to remind people of what horrors happened there and help ensure that these atrocities are never repeated.

▲ Today, visitors to Dachau concentration camp learn about the terrible crimes that took place there.

After 1945, disputes between the Allies and the Soviet Union led to the establishment of two separate countries in Germany. West Germany (the Federal Republic of Germany) was supported by the USA and the Western allies. East Germany (the German Democratic Republic) was supported by the Soviet Union and its communist allies. Bonn became the capital of West Germany and East Berlin became the capital of East Germany.

THE COMMUNIST EAST

East Germany therefore became a communist country. Its secret police, the Stasi, were hated for the control they exerted over people's lives. The Stasi encouraged family members to spy and inform on one another. East German farms

▼ Between 1961 and 1989, the Brandenburg Gate in Berlin, shown here lit up at night, was the dividing line between East and West Germany.

were collectivized (organized into large, state-owned units); industry was also tightly controlled by the state (government). The state set targets for industry, agriculture and all aspects of life. In agriculture, the aim of this was to make the country independent, but economic growth was slow because of poor organization, insufficient finance for investment and a lack of natural resources. In contrast, West Germany and other Western European countries received economic aid from the USA to help them recover from the Second World War. West Germany therefore enjoyed rapid economic growth.

West Germany's economic success brought a flood of refugees from East Germany. In 1961, to prevent further loss of their population, the East Germans were forced to build a wall dividing East and West Berlin. The situation remained more or less the same, until 1989.

▲ At Checkpoint Charlie, a crossing point in the Berlin Wall, there is a memorial to the East Germans shot or arrested trying to flee to the West.

In the autumn of that year there were mass demonstrations by groups opposed to communist rule, and the end of a divided Germany swiftly followed. The Berlin Wall was torn down and, in November 1989, the frontier between East and West Germany was opened. In August 1990, a Unification Treaty was signed between East and West Germany.

AFTER 1990

In 1990, the process of reunifying Germany began in earnest. The West German chancellor, Helmut Kohl, was the driving force behind the privatization of industry in the eastern regions and the reinstatement of Berlin as Germany's capital city. Throughout the 1990s, Germany rebuilt many of the railways, roads and factories of the eastern regions that had been so neglected in the previous twenty years. In 1999, Germany joined the European Monetary Union and was strongly in favour of introducing a common currency. On 1 January 2002, the first Euro notes and coins began to circulate.

In 1992, with other NATO (see page 35) countries, Germany took part in the invasion of Bosnia to restore peace to a region plagued by civil strife. However, when coalition forces from the USA and the UK invaded Iraq in 2003 to overthrow Saddam Hussein, Germany spoke out against the move. Since then, Germany has campaigned to withdraw troops from Iraq as soon as possible. Germany is also one of the nations involved in the campaign to write off the debt of the world's eighteen poorest nations.

? Did you know?

In 1948, the Soviet Union blockaded West Berlin for nearly a year. This was the time of the Cold War – a period of intense and growing mistrust between West (essentially the USA and Western Europe) and East (the Soviet Union). The Western powers organized a major airlift of 300,000 flights to keep Berlin supplied with food and fuel.

CHAPTER 3

Landscape and Climate

Germany has many different landscapes, from broad plains to high mountains and deep valleys. The landscape of the north and north-east of the country tends to be flat, rising in height towards the Alpine mountains of the south. Most of Germany's rivers, such as the Elbe and the Rhine, flow north or north-west, following the relief of the land. They drain into the Baltic or the North Sea. The exception is the Danube, which flows eastwards into Austria. The Rhine is the most important river in the country because it is so long and is navigable by barges for much of its length. It rises in the Swiss Alps and flows for 1,320 km (820 miles) to the Netherlands, where it drains into the North Sea. The Rhine forms part of Germany's frontier with France.

THE EUROPEAN PLAIN

The North Sea coast of Germany is flat. Here the sea is shallow, which means that in most winters it freezes. Sandy beaches and sand spits are found along this part of the coast. Further east are German-owned islands in the Baltic, of which the largest is Rügen, famous for its chalk cliffs. Most of northern Germany forms part of the European Plain, which extends from France to Russia. This area consists of low plains, shallow lakes and marshes.

▼ The Baltic coast consists of long, sandy beaches flanked by low, chalk hills. Despite the cold winds and cool sea, it is a favourite holiday destination for many Germans.

THE CENTRAL UPLANDS

To the south are the Central Uplands, including the area of the Eifel, with its famous lakes that fill the craters of extinct volcanoes, and the valleys of the rivers Moselle and Rhine. The Rhine cuts through the Central Uplands to form a gorge where picturesque castles are perched upon clifftops overlooking the rivers. Vines grow on the warm valley slopes and the grapes are used to make world famous wines.

▲ Castles like this were built above the River Rhine to protect local people and to extract tolls from vessels using the river.

 Did you know?

The lowest point in Germany is 3.54 m (11.6 feet) below sea level at Neuendorf bei Wilster, and the highest point is the 2,963-metre (9,721-foot) Zugspitze Mountain in the Alps.

Focus on: Flooding

With so many major rivers, large parts of Germany are affected by flooding. This usually happens during spring, when the mountain snows melt, or in autumn, when heavy rains swell the rivers. In 1997, the River Oder in eastern Germany burst its banks and flooded the surrounding farmland and towns. In 2002, the River Elbe rose from its normal summer level of 2 m (6 feet 6ins) to 9.4 m (30 feet 2 ins), a new record high, and overflowed on to the surrounding flood plain. Buildings in Dresden were flooded and 12,000 people had to be evacuated from their homes. The mayor of Dresden estimated that it would take hundreds of millions of Euros to repair the damage. As the tide of floodwater swept further downriver, another 8,000 people had to be evacuated from the town of Torgau.

THE ALPS

South of the Central Uplands are the Alps, high rugged mountains rising to over 2,000 m (6,562 feet), some of which are covered with snow and ice in winter. The lower slopes of the mountains are thickly wooded. Areas like this, such as the Black Forest of Bavaria, give way on the lowest slopes to meadows. Blue gentians and other wild flowers used to be found in these meadows, but the use of chemicals in farming has reduced their numbers.

INFLUENCES ON THE CLIMATE

Germany's central position in Europe means that it is where the warm, wet winds from the west meet the cold, dry winds from the east. As a result, weather can vary widely from day to day and from year to year. In a severe winter, temperatures may fall well below freezing and stay there for several weeks, especially if the land is covered with snow and there is a persistent high-pressure system over central Europe. The following year may see a mild, wet winter with relatively little snow. Conditions also vary from region to region. On average, the western areas have milder winters

(0°C, 32°F) and cooler summers (15°C, 62°F) than the eastern regions, which have cold winters (-4°C, 23°F) and hot, sunny summers (20°C, 72°F).

The climate of northern and western Germany is affected by the moderating influence of the sea, which gives milder winters and cooler summers than areas further east. Winters in the east may be so cold that the rivers, lakes and seas freeze over for several weeks. The central and eastern parts of the country have a shorter growing season and more days of frost. For example, Aachen has only 42 days of frost per year while Berlin has 90 days. Altitude also affects temperatures which fall by about 1°C (1.8 °F) for every 150 metres (492 ft) of altitude. This is called the lapse rate. So, for example, the plateau of the River Rhine is 3°C to 4°C colder than the nearby city of Cologne, which is

▼ On the rich, volcanic soils of western Germany, vines are grown in straight rows to make it easier for farmers to pick the grapes and prune and care for the plants.

around 455 m lower. The area around Freiburg in south-west Germany is known for being the sunniest place in the country.

Germany receives an average of between 600–800 mm (23.5–31.5 inches) of precipitation (rain or snow) per year, but this varies significantly from place to place. High areas, such as the Black Forest and the Harz Mountains, receive more than 1,200 mm (47 inches) per year. The driest places are in the south and east, where the Alps protect the land from rain-bearing winds.

There is heavy winter snowfall in the Alps in the south. When the snow melts in spring it often causes flooding of rivers like the Rhine and the Danube, which rise in this area.

▼ The Alps in Germany are high enough to retain snow well into the spring, so are attractive areas for late skiing.

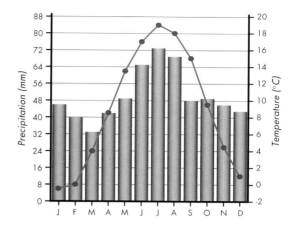

▲ Average monthly climate conditions in Berlin

 Did you know?

In May, some parts of central Germany have a brief cool spell, which is called 'the three ice saints'. Each spring, a warm, dry wind known as the *Fohn* visits southern Germany and it can melt several feet of snow within a few hours.

CHAPTER 4

Population and Settlements

Germany has a total population of 82.5 million. Of this total, around 15 million live in the region that formerly comprised East Germany, an area that is still less densely populated than the west. Most Germans live in villages and small towns; even the largest cities are modest in size compared with other world cities. Around 27 million people live in cities with more than 100,000 inhabitants, 49 million live in small towns of between 2,000 and 100,000 people, and the rest live in the countryside.

POPULATION DENSITY

The most densely populated regions are Greater Berlin, the Ruhr industrial area (near the border with the Netherlands), and the areas around Frankfurt-am-Main, Wiesbaden and Mannheim. Germany has only nineteen cities with more than 300,000 people, of which only two (Berlin and Frankfurt-am-Main) are in the former East Germany. Germany's largest cities are Berlin (3.3 million people), Hamburg (2.7 million) and Stuttgart (2.7 million).

Following reunification in 1990, the population of Berlin was expected to grow rapidly to 8 million by 2010. But many young families have left Berlin since 1990 in search of a better quality of life in villages and small towns in the countryside. It now looks as though the population of Berlin will remain at its present size for the foreseeable future. In Germany as a whole, many people are leaving large towns and cities for the cleaner, healthier environment of

▼ On the face of it, Germany's financial centre, Frankfurt-am-Main, looks like a typical modern city with office blocks and skyscrapers. But many of its buildings, including the old Jewish quarter, date back several centuries.

the countryside. City dwellers are buying up farms and cottages close to towns. Often they then sell off the land and redesign the buildings. During the day, these villages are very quiet because everyone is away at work. The villages only come to life in the evenings, when people return to their homes.

POPULATION GROWTH

The German birth rate is 8.6 births per 1,000 population, and the death rate is 10.34 deaths per 1,000 population. This means that the population would be in decline were it not for some small-scale immigration. Even so, overall growth is slow at 0.1 per cent.

The rate of growth has been slow for more than fifteen years, which means that Germany has an ageing population. The German population structure is typical of many western European countries where the birth rate has been falling for the last fifty years. This high percentage of older people is causing serious concern, because in future there will be relatively few younger people

▲ Even relatively small German villages, like this one near Alpirsbach, have zones for recreational activities to improve the health of young people.

Population data

- Population: 82.5 million
- Population 0-14 yrs: 15% .
- Population 15-64 yrs: 68% .
- Population 65+ yrs: 17%
- Population growth rate: 0.1%
- Population density: 236.2 per sq km/611.9 per sq mile
- Urban population: 88%
- Major cities: Berlin 3,328,000
  Hamburg 2,686,000
  Stuttgart 2,705,000

Source: United Nations and World Bank

 Did you know?

Between 1945 and 1990, ten million people fled from East to West Germany.

to support many older people. Another problem is the question of who will pay for the health care, care homes, pensions and other requirements of an older population. A range of solutions has been proposed, among them the idea of offering tax cuts to encourage people to have larger families, and relaxing the immigration laws to allow people from abroad to come and work in Germany.

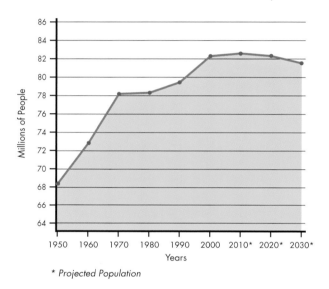

* Projected Population

▲ Population growth 1950-2030

GUEST WORKERS

Germany has become home to many different ethnic groups. In the nineteenth century, Polish miners came to Germany for work. More recently, the very rapid economic growth in the 1950s and 1960s meant that immigrants were needed to provide labour for German industry. The German government encouraged guest workers (*Gastarbeiter)* to come to Germany from countries such as Turkey, Morocco and Yugoslavia. A guest worker is someone who moves to a country to live and work for more than one year. These workers came to find better paid jobs and a better quality of life than were available in their own countries and they came to do the more menial jobs

that Germans did not want to do, such as bus driving and garbage disposal. Guest workers became permanent residents, but were not citizens (see panel opposite). In many cases, whole families moved to Germany. By 1973, there were 2.3 million guest workers in the country, and by 2004 the number had grown to 3.2 million.

In the 1970s, economic recession ended the process of immigration, but most guest workers stayed on in Germany. Now they form an important part of German society and are counted in the census. The Turkish ethnic community, which consists of more than two million people, is the largest in Germany. It is followed by Yugoslavs (i.e. Serbs) with 715,000 people. Germany has also become a centre for asylum seekers who come from countries such as the former Yugoslavia or from other central European countries, such as Albania. The

? Did you know?

Since 1990, 2.5 million people have settled in Germany from Kazakhastan and other parts of Eastern Europe and have been allowed to become citizens.

▼ These musicians from Turkey earn a living by playing for passers-by in Frankfurt.

asylum seekers must undergo a strict application system before they are allowed to stay in Germany and some are either sent back to their country of origin or deported to another country.

 Did you know?

80,000 people seek asylum in Germany each year, but only about 10,000 are successful.

▼ A fire at a mosque in Usingen, built to serve the members of the local Muslim community. The fire might have been accidental, or the result of a racist arson attack.

Focus on: Citizenship

In 1999, a law was passed to update Germany's citizenship laws. The old laws dated back to 1913 and they defined nationality according to blood not birthplace. This meant that the children of guest workers could not become German citizens and therefore could not vote in elections. From 2000, anyone born to non-German parents is allowed to have 'provisional citizenship'. Then, at the age of 23, they must decide whether to retain the nationality of their parents or to become full German citizens.

CHAPTER 5

Government and Politics

Germany is a constitutional democracy with a federal system of government similar to that of the USA. The head of state is the federal president, who has little political power but represents the country on national matters. The federal president is elected for five years and can only be re-elected once. The chancellor holds the real power. He or she appoints ministers to the government and, with them, runs the key elements of government such as health, education and defence.

The country is divided up into 16 states, or *Länder*. The people of each *Länder* have strong feelings about retaining their own independence and identity. For example, many people in Bavaria refer to themselves as Bavarians first and Germans second. Each *Länder* has considerable power over its own affairs.

THE GERMAN PARLIAMENT

Since 1999, the German parliament has met in the imposing Reichstag building in Berlin. There are two main houses of parliament: the Bundestag and the Bundesrat. The Bundestag elects the chancellor and initiates most legislation. A simple majority is needed for most laws to be passed. A two-thirds majority in both houses is needed to bring about changes to the constitution.

▼ This special session of the German Bundestag was convened in 2002 to receive an address by US president, George Bush (centre, standing at podium).

About half the Bundestag is made up of candidates elected directly from each *Länder*. The other half is made up of delegates appointed by political parties. The reason for this is to prevent too many local issues dominating the political agenda. For a party to be represented in the Bundestag, it has to win 5 per cent of the vote at a national election or have three directly elected MPs. It can then appoint non-elected delegates to the Bundestag.

The Bundesrat is the upper house in the German parliament. It is part of the legislature – the law-making body in government. Its members are made up of delegates who represent the 16 *Länder*. They are appointed by parliament.

ELECTIONS

Elections are held every four years and the chancellor can only be replaced if there is a new

 The seat of the German Bundestag is the Reichstag. One of the building's main features is the glistening glass dome that covers the plenary hall.

? Did you know?

Germany's National Unity Day is 3 October. It celebrates the political and cultural bringing together of the German people.

candidate for the post with an assured majority. In practice, the chancellor is the leader of the party that wins most of the votes at the election. Voting is not compulsory, but the turnout is usually about 80 per cent. This is considerably higher than in much of the rest of Western Europe. Germans realize the importance of voting and see it as part of their civic duty. German women have had the vote since 1918 and are well represented in German politics. In 2004, they made up 26 per cent of the Bundestag.

The chief political parties are the Christian Democratic Union (CDU), also known as the Christian Democrat Party (CDP), the Social Democratic Party (SPD), the Green Party (Alliance 90/The Greens) and the Free Democratic Party (FDP).

ISSUES EMERGING FROM REUNIFICATION

Although Germany was officially reunified in 1990, the real task of bringing East and West Germany together was still to come. Helmut Kohl, the German chancellor and head of the CDP political party, drove the process along. He oversaw huge changes, especially in former East Germany where industries were privatized and modernized. Kohl reassured the people in neighbouring states, such as Poland, who were worried about the growing political and economic power of the new Germany. Kohl

was also the driving force behind the move of the parliament from Bonn back to Berlin. During the 1990s, the role of women began to change in the former East Germany. Before reunification, about 90 per cent of East German women were employed, or in training programmes. This was because there was a serious labour shortage caused by the flight of many young men to West Germany. However, after reunification, about 63 per cent of these women were out of work as a result of the closure of factories and offices which could not compete with the larger and more efficient firms in the West. Since then, some women have found work in offices and shops but, in

▼ The city of Dresden was very badly damaged by Allied bombing during the Second World War. However, it has been carefully rebuilt since 1990 using the original plans.

2003, 42 per cent of the total female labour force was still out of work in the former East Germany.

Since reunification the government has established programmes throughout the country to help women, especially those with young children, to return to work. A disproportionate number of women are still out of work in the eastern region, however. In 2002, opinion polls in the eastern areas suggested that 13 per cent of employed women placed more importance on their careers than on having a family. This is similar to the figure of 14 per cent of women who were asked the same question in the western areas of the country. However, women in the east and the west differed in their attitudes towards self-development, such as training to gain new skills or other forms of personal development. In the east, women seek self-development mainly to earn more money and achieve a higher standard of living. In the west, women pursue it more for reasons of personal fulfillment.

One of the most difficult issues to emerge from reunification was that of abortion. In East Germany, abortion had been legal up to 12 weeks after conception. Laws in West Germany were stricter. After 1995, abortion in the new Germany was declared illegal (with medical exceptions) but it was not a criminal act if carried out within 12 weeks of conception and with compulsory counselling.

Focus on: The Green Party

The Green Party (Alliance 90/The Greens) was founded in the 1970s. The Greens won their first seat in the state parliament of Bremen in 1979. The membership grew in the 1980s when the Greens became part of the peace and ecological movements, which supported world peace and increased ecological awareness. In 1993, the party joined forces with Alliance 90, a confederation of civil rights groups from former East Germany. The high point for the Greens was 1998, when they won 47 seats and formed a coalition government with the SPD. Since then, the Greens have had a less powerful voice in government but have still been able to secure a deal with the energy industry to phase out nuclear power by 2030 and replace it with renewable energy.

▶ Green Party member, Karl Schliebermilch, travels to and from the Reichstag by bicycle to demonstrate the use of non-polluting transport.

CHAPTER 6

Energy and Resources

Germany's industrial growth has been fuelled by energy generated from fossil fuels such as coal, oil and natural gas. Germany used to be rich in both black coal and brown coal. (The latter is called lignite; it has a lower energy value than black coal and creates a lot of air pollution.) The main black coalfield is the Ruhr in the western part of the country. From the 1890s onwards, the Ruhr provided the energy for rapidly growing German industries. Coal is still produced there, but in much smaller quantities than in the past. This is because, in the last thirty years or so, mines have become uneconomic and have closed down. Brown coal is still used to generate electricity in the eastern regions, but it is more valuable as a raw material for the chemicals industry so less of it is burned in power stations today.

NATURAL GAS

Fossil fuels are used to generate 62 per cent of all electricity in Germany. However, most of this is generated not by burning coal but by burning natural gas. Natural gas is the fuel of choice because it is cleaner than coal and does not contribute to acid rain in the same way. Germany produces small amounts of natural gas and oil in the north-western areas, but the majority of supplies are imported from Russia via long pipelines.

▼ This photo shows one of the more modern coalmines near Saarbrucken in Germany. Coal seams are deeper and more fractured than they used to be, so mines have been modernized. Mechanized coal-cutting equipment is used to keep costs down.

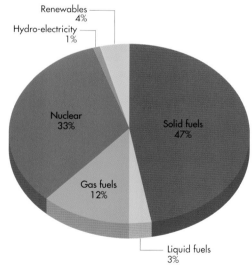

▲ Wind farms like these are becoming a familiar sight in parts of Germany. They make a valuable contribution to generating non-polluting electricity.

▲ Energy generation by source

Focus on: Hydro-electric power

Hydro-electric power (HEP) provides 1 per cent of Germany's electricity. HEP stations are located along the fast-flowing rivers to be found in the Alpine areas of southern Germany. Here the mountains provide the naturally steep gradients necessary for HEP generation. A few other HEP stations have been built along the major rivers, such as the Rhine and Elbe. Hydro-electric power stations are expensive to build but cheap to run because the fuel (water) is free. HEP is also popular because it causes little or no pollution, unlike most other types of power.

 Did you know?

Germany has 19 nuclear power stations. In the 1990s, anti-nuclear protests were so widespread that trains carrying nuclear waste were threatened by angry protesters. 20,000 police were employed to protect the trains from attack.

NUCLEAR POWER

Nuclear power provides 33 per cent of the country's electricity. Germany began building nuclear power stations during the 1970s, when it seemed that there might be a shortage of coal or oil in future. Nuclear power stations have been very controversial in Germany because of the dangers of possible radiation leaks. Other dangers have also become more apparent, such as the problem of how to dispose of the radioactive waste safely.

No part of the country wants to act as a storage point for the nuclear waste, so it is currently stored on the site of nuclear power plants. Safe, long-term storage remains a huge problem. The phasing out of nuclear power stations only partly solves the problem because it still leaves the issue of how to dispose of the nuclear waste. The first nuclear power station to be closed down in Germany was shut in 2004.

RENEWABLE ENERGY

The remaining 4 per cent of Germany's energy is derived from wind and solar power. The government is keen to increase electricity generation by renewable sources such as this to 10 per cent by 2020. Wind energy is an important alternative source of electricity generation in Germany. Modern wind turbines have very large rotors of 60 m (197 feet) and the tips of the blades can travel at up to 400 km per hour (250 mph)! Wind turbines are usually built in clusters, called wind farms. In Germany these are located mostly along the Baltic and North Sea coasts and there are plans to construct some offshore wind farms. People who live near the farms have criticized them because of their noise and visual impact. But wind farms cause no air pollution and do not contribute to acid rain or global warming.

▲ These houses in Heidelberg have been built using solar panels (visible on the roofs) to heat the domestic hot water systems.

SOLAR POWER

Solar power is generated by the Sun's rays falling on to silicon cells, which generate electricity. The use of solar energy on a large scale tends to be very expensive. Solar cells are arranged in panels, which are usually sited on the roofs of buildings. In Germany there is a programme called 'one million roofs' which aims to install solar panels in one million homes by 2010. Solar cells are not very efficient, so research into improving them continues, but they clearly have a future in the sunniest parts of Germany, such as Freiburg in the south-west.

OTHER RESOURCES

In the past, much of Germany was densely forested, but over the years large areas of trees have been felled to provide fuel and building timber. This occurred on a large scale in the eighteenth century, when industries such as glass-making needed timber for charcoal that was used to heat sand and convert it to glass. The cleared areas were replanted with fast-growing conifers. This meant that some deciduous woodland areas, such as the Harz Mountains, were changed into coniferous forests. Despite this, Germany still has large areas of deciduous woodland, such as parts of the Black Forest, which are home to industries such as woodcarving and timber production.

Another resource is fishing. Fleets operate along the North and Baltic Sea coasts of Germany, but they have been cut back in recent years as part of an attempt to conserve fish stocks, especially in the North Sea.

Germany used to be rich in minerals such as iron ore, sulphur, lead and zinc. Few of these are still mined because over the years it has become more expensive to extract them from greater and greater depths.

Energy data

- Energy consumption as % of world total: 3.6%
- Energy consumption by sector (% of total),
  Industry: 34
  Transportation: 28
  Agriculture: 1
  Services: 10
  Residential: 27
- CO_2 emissions as % of world total: 3.5
- CO_2 emissions per capita in tonnes p.a.:10

Source: World Resources Institute

 Did you know?

In Germany, over one million trees are cut each year to make timber and wood pulp.

▼ Germany spends over $12 million on timber imports from the rest of the world. This means that the timber harvest in the Black Forest, shown below, is important in reducing the need for imports.

CHAPTER 7

Economy and Income

Agriculture is one of Germany's smallest industries, but it is one of its most important. Although it accounts for only 2.8 per cent of employment and 1 per cent of the Gross National Income (GNI), agriculture is central to the country's economy. This is because Germany produces 53 per cent of its own food from highly efficient farms. There are still many small farms of fewer than 10 hectares (25 acres), worked by part-time farmers who usually have another job as well as farming. Nearly 60 per cent of farmers have a second job. However, there are also some large farms that are run on strict business lines to gain the maximum return for the input of time, money and expertise.

FARMING ANIMALS

Dairy farming, the production of milk, butter and cheese, is well suited to the cool conditions found throughout most of Germany. In the drier areas, wheat, barley and sugar beet are grown. Conditions are warmer in the southern parts of the country and here maize is grown as feed for cattle and pigs. Most pigs are reared in livestock units, which consist of large sheds with huge grain silos next to them. These provide the feed for sufficient animals to meet the German population's demand for pork and sausages (*Wurst*).

Economic data

- Gross National Income (GNI) in US$: 2,084,631,000,000
- World rank by GNI: 3
- GNI per capita in US$: 25,250
- World rank by GNI per capita: 22
- Economic growth: 0%

Source: World Bank

Did you know?

Germany has over 22 million pigs, 19 million cattle and 1.2 million sheep. The number of farms in Germany decreased from 2.1 million in 1950 to 666,000 in 2002. Pork is the most popular meat among the German people followed by veal, chicken and beef.

▼ Since reunification, the mechanization of farming in eastern parts of Germany has resulted in greater efficiency and higher yields.

▲ In order to make wine, the ripe grapes are picked from the vines and loaded into trucks.

WINE PRODUCTION

Germany is an important producer and exporter of wine. Most vineyards are on south facing slopes along the valley of the River Rhine and its tributaries. Over the years the steep hillsides have been terraced to provide level ground on which vines can be grown. So that consumers can tell one from the other, Rhine wine is sold in brown bottles and wine from the Moselle area is sold in green bottles. Germany is also a major producer of beer. The barley and hops are grown throughout the county and are used to produce high quality beers.

CO-OPERATIVES IN THE EAST

Prior to reunification, the eastern areas of Germany were cultivated by large farming co-operatives controlled by the government. The government told farmers what to grow, when to plough and when to plant. This system was very inefficient because it lacked adequate resources, such as tractors and combine harvesters, to work the land. There was little incentive for people to work hard because they did not own the land, so they did not stand to benefit directly if production increased. After 1990, the co-operative farms were broken up or sold to groups of farmers. These farmers are now free to make their own decisions about what to grow and where and when to grow it.

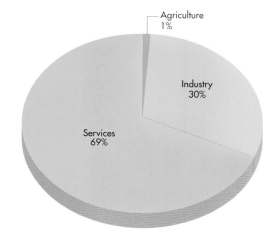

Agriculture 1%

Industry 30%

Services 69%

▲ Contribution by sector to national income

ENGINEERING AND MANUFACTURING

Germany is one of the world's biggest economies. German engineering has a reputation for designing high quality products, and German industry produces high-tech goods such as cameras, lenses and cars. Among the best-known German brands are Mercedes, BMW, Volkswagen, Zeiss and Bosch. Manufacturing industries employ around 33 per cent of the German workforce (about two million people) in mainly medium sized companies with fewer than 100 employees. Germany's manufacturers produce a range of consumer goods such as television sets, computers, washing machines, refrigerators and microwave ovens.

Heavy industries producing cars, vans, trucks, ships and a wide range of machinery are still important in Germany. Many of the goods they produce are exported all over the world.

▼ The Mercedes car production factory is one of the largest and most modern in the world. Many people from Europe travel to the factory to collect the car they have bought and to take a tour of the factory.

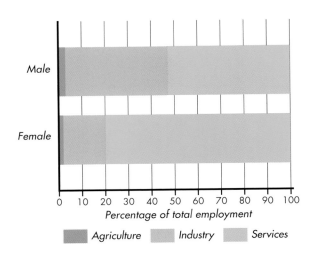

▲ Labour force by sector and gender

  Did you know?

The original Volkswagen beetle car was developed under Adolf Hitler during the 1930s. The vehicle continued in production until the 1980s, when it was replaced by a new design of beetle.

Focus on: Eastern Germany

By 1989, over 80 per cent of the workforce in East Germany were employed in state controlled industries. After reunification it became clear that ageing equipment was hampering industry in the east. Industry was also overstaffed, subsidized and inefficient. After 1990 many industries were sold, but West German firms were reluctant to invest, so many of the eastern firms were sold to East German managers. New machinery was introduced and factories were re-equipped, but the cost has been high. The east is still only 70 per cent as productive as the west.

CHEMICALS INDUSTRY

The German chemicals industry first developed on the brown coalfields because they supplied the raw material for the industry. However, soon oil became the new raw material of the industry. Chemical works were built along the rivers Rhine and Elbe and the oil was imported to the works by barge or pipeline. The chemicals industry is very important to the German economy and it produces everything from pharmaceuticals to plastics and paint.

ENVIRONMENTAL PROTECTION

Almost one million people work in industries connected with environmental protection (as many as work in the automobile industry). Germany has 18 per cent of the world market in this field. Much of this environmental work concerns the management of waste, which is a fast growing sector of the economy. Germany is a leading producer of specialist vehicles that are designed to collect waste, such as green waste, paper, glass and textiles, for recycling. Germany also produces most of the equipment used to measure concentrations of pollutants in air and water and to monitor traffic flow in major cities.

SERVICE INDUSTRIES

Over 69 per cent of the workforce is involved in service industries such as transport, retailing, finance, professional and public services. Some of the people employed in service industries work in offices, many of which are located in large tower blocks. The skylines of modern cities, such as Berlin and Frankfurt, are dominated by these office blocks, which are usually located close to city centre shops. This concentration of offices leads to traffic congestion, so some new office parks have been built on the edge of cities to provide office employment away from city centres. Other offices are based in more modest buildings, sometimes in the older parts of towns and cities. Tourism is another very important service industry. It employs people who cater for winter sports holidays, city breaks and vacations in the lakes and mountains.

 Did you know?

Although Berlin is the capital of Germany, only 11 of the 500 largest corporations are based in Berlin, with 50 in Hamburg and another 33 in Munich.

▲ Planners in cities like Berlin try to make sure that modern chemical factories like this have trees planted around them to reduce their impact on the landscape.

CHAPTER 8

Global Connections

Germany is an important member of the European Union (EU), an alliance of 25 European countries. In 1957, six countries, including Germany and France, signed up to the European Economic Community (EEC), the forerunner of the EU. The alliance between France and Germany was in part an attempt to move away from the conflicts of the past and establish a new, positive relationship at the heart of Europe.

PROMOTING TRADE

An early aim of the Community was to promote trade between its members. It was very successful in doing this, so much so that other countries joined the EEC and the group's interests expanded beyond trade to include social and judicial co-operation. In 1991 the EEC's name was changed to European Union to reflect its wider remit. Since 1991, the EU has become a much broader organization, with its own parliament elected by the member

Did you know?

The city of Strasbourg is half in Germany and half in France. For this reason it was chosen as the location for the headquarters of the EU.

▼ This photo shows one branch of the headquarters of the European Union in Strasbourg. The other branch is in Brussels, Belgium.

countries and a president and commissioners who are responsible for its day-to-day running. Germany occupies a central position in Europe and has a long history of contacts with Eastern Europe. It therefore plays an important role in fostering trade and investment in Eastern Europe and was influential in encouraging East European countries such as the Czech Republic, Slovenia and Poland to become members of the EU. These countries eventually joined the EU in May 2004, together with nine other nations.

▲ The European Central Bank is located in Frankfurt, Germany. The photo shows a structure depicting the symbol of the Euro, outside the bank.

NATO

Germany is also a key member of the North Atlantic Treaty Organization (NATO). This was formed at the end of the Second World War to help to defend Western Europe against the spread of communism from the Soviet Union. After 1945, a period of Cold War existed between the Soviet Union (and its communist allies) and the West (Britain, the USA and their allies, for example, France). Following the collapse of the former Soviet Union in 1991, the threat from communism in Eastern Europe lessened and the role of NATO changed. The countries in NATO now provide troops for NATO activities, such as peacekeeping in Bosnia and the former Yugoslavia, and German troops are a vital part of these operations.

The strength of Germany's economy means it is important to European and world trade. About 60 per cent of all Germany's trade is with other EU countries. Germany's main trading partner is France, followed by the USA, the UK and Italy. Other trading partners include the Netherlands, Austria and Belgium.

 Did you know?

The European Central Bank controls the Euro zone – the number of countries in which the Euro is the currency.

Focus on: The Single European Currency

In 1999, Germany became one of the twelve EU countries to form the European Monetary Union (EMU). In the EMU, member states ceased to use the old currencies, such as the deutsche mark, and instead use the Euro as their only currency. In 2002, Euro notes and coins entered circulation for the first time in these twelve countries. There was much opposition to abandoning the deutsche mark as the unit of currency in Germany because it had been very stable. However, the success of the Euro meant that by 2004 most Germans were happy to have abandoned the deutsche mark.

LINKS WITH RUSSIA

Germany is particularly interested in developing trade links with Russia. Much of Germany's oil and natural gas comes from Russia via the Friendship Pipeline, which runs from Siberia through Poland to Germany, and beyond, to France and the UK. In return, Russia is keen to gain access to the technological expertise that is characteristic of most German industry. In particular, Germany manufactures the high quality valves and control equipment that Russia needs for the building of even longer pipelines to carry oil from its Siberian oilfields. Russia has such large reserves of oil and gas that it will play a major role in the future of energy in the world. Germany is eager to build links with Russia so that it can be involved in this process.

▼ The containerization of the transport of a wide range of goods has led to the rapid growth of dock areas like this in Hamburg.

EXPORTS AND IMPORTS

Germany's main exports are machinery, vehicles, chemicals and metals. Goods such as basic steel, tyres and vehicle panels are imported into Germany so that more complex and valuable manufactured goods such as cars, cameras and electrical equipment can be made in German factories. Many of these high value goods are exported. Germany's main imports are machinery, vehicles, chemicals, foodstuffs, textiles and metals. This pattern of trade shows that Germany is an advanced economy –producing many consumer goods, processing imported semi-finished manufactured goods and then re-exporting the finished goods.

LINKS WITH THE FAR EAST

Germany is keen to develop closer links with the countries of the Far East such as China and Japan. China has emerged as a major manufacturing nation in the last ten years, with very low costs based on low wage rates.

German companies have realized the importance of importing some manufactured goods from China and switching their own production to higher tech and more expensive products. At the same time, German firms are moving some of their production to China to gain access to the Chinese market and take advantage of the lower wages and looser environmental protection laws.

Germany is an important country in terms of international finance. The Stock Exchange (Bourse) in Frankfurt handles thousands of transactions, selling and buying shares in companies from all over the world. The Bourse has grown so rapidly over the last few years that it now rivals London as the financial capital of Europe. German banks are also very important to the European and world banking system, and deal with millions of accounts from all over the world.

Did you know?

In 2002, Germany's exports were worth US$608 billion and imports were worth US$487.3 billion.

▲ A share trader uses two phones to place orders in front of the German financial prices index at Frankfurt-am-Main's Stock Exchange (Bourse).

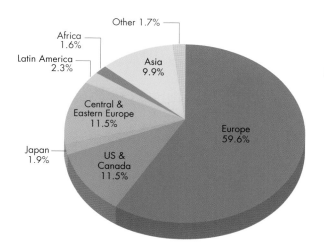

▲ Destination of exports by major trading region

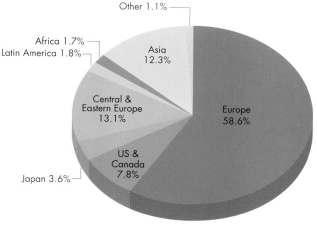

▲ Origin of imports by major trading region

CHAPTER 9

Transport and Communications

Germany has some of the best motorways (*autobahnen*) in the world. The motorways were first built during the 1930s as a means of moving troops quickly and easily around the country. During the Second World War many *autobahnen* were damaged, but they were rebuilt and extended in West Germany after 1945. In East Germany the communist government did little to repair the motorways, but progress has been rapid since 1990. Other roads in Germany are also good and provide links with most parts of the country. New road building continues, especially in the east, to connect more remote areas with the rest of Germany.

▲ Germany has excellent motorways: this is important because Germany's central position in Europe means that most trans-European routes have to pass through the country.

GOODS TRANSPORTATION

An increasing number of goods are transported by road. They include even some heavy, bulky materials such as steel and timber. The government is trying to prevent the worst effects of the rapid expansion of road transport by recommending an integrated transport system. This involves the movement of goods by rail or water, followed by their transfer to road for the final leg of the journey.

RAILWAYS

German railways (*Deutsche Bahn*) operate a fast and frequent service between 7,000 main towns and cities. Germany is a big country, so the railways are particularly important in connecting all the different areas. Since 1990, the network has been developed to integrate the eastern regions with the rest of the country. New high speed links, which cut travel times by up to 30 per cent, have been built connecting Berlin to cities such as Hanover and Munich. The railways are also important in terms of the transport of goods. New, more powerful locomotives can carry larger loads over longer distances at greater speeds. Rail transport is ideal for heavy, bulky materials such as chemicals, cars and machinery, and is certain to play an important role within an integrated transport system.

Some of the major cities, such as Berlin, Frankfurt, Munich and Hamburg, have underground railways. Berlin has two systems: the older overground S-Bahn with 13 lines which has been modernized, and the underground U-Bahn with 10 lines, which carries an estimated 450,000 people each day. These railway systems transport people to and from work, and are valuable in reducing the volume of traffic in city centres. There are also a few privately run cog railways, which take trains up some of the country's steepest mountains.

▲ Railways are still an important means of transport in Germany. Lines have been electrified and modernized in an attempt to reduce journey times.

Transport & communications data

- 📁 Total roads: 230,735 km/143,286 miles
- 📁 Total paved roads: 230,735 km/143,286 miles
- 📁 Total unpaved roads: 0 km/0 miles
- 📁 Total railways: 46,039 km/28,608 miles
- 📁 Major airports: 550
- 📁 Cars per 1,000 people: 516
- 📁 Mobile phones per 1,000 people: 727
- 📁 Personal computers per 1,000 people: 431
- 📁 Internet users per 1,000 people: 412

Source: World Bank and CIA World Factbook

 Did you know?

There are 46,039 km (28,608 m) of railway track in Germany, of which 21,000 km (13,049 m) are electrified to give faster journeys and enable the railways to compete with the airlines. The modern Inter City Express (ICE) trains travel at speeds of up to 280km/h (174 mph).

AIR TRAVEL

Domestic air travel is very popular in Germany because of the size of the country and the relatively low cost. Most major cities have at least one airport, and the main national airline is Lufthansa (although it is not government owned), based at Frankfurt. There are also smaller airlines offering services to other countries, to regional cities and to the North Frisian Islands. Air travel is ideal for passengers who are in a hurry, and for goods such as jewels, that are valuable in relation to their weight, and for perishable goods such as flowers and fruit. Berlin and Frankfurt are the two main international airports.

▼ Munich airport: the growth of air transport is based on the development of business travel and the growth of tourism, especially with the introduction of low cost airlines.

WATER TRANSPORT

Where speed of transportation is less important than cost, water transport is a favoured option. Heavy, bulky goods such as coal, oil, iron ore, timber and steel tend to be transported by water, which is the best way of moving these goods cheaply and easily around the country. One of the largest industrial areas in the world has grown up along the River Rhine, in the Ruhr industrial zone around Duisburg. The industry in this area is based on local coal, and imported raw materials such as oil and iron ore transported by water from Rotterdam. Large barges use the rivers, especially the Rhine and the Elbe, to carry goods from ports such as Hamburg to the interior of the country. They also carry goods in the opposite direction, for export. Smaller vessels carry tourists along rivers such as the Rhine, Moselle and the Elbe and, in summer, tourist steamers run on Lake Constance in south Germany.

▲ A barge is used to transport a heavy, bulky load of coal on the River Rhine.

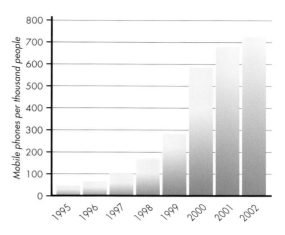

▲ Mobile phone use, 1995-2002

TELECOMMUNICATIONS NETWORKS

Germany has one of the world's most advanced telecommunications systems. Huge amounts of money have been spent modernizing it in former East Germany to bring it up to the standard of the rest of the country and to integrate the two systems. There is an extensive system of telephone exchanges connected by modern networks of fibre-optic cable. There are also cellular (mobile) telephone systems (with 727 phones per 1,000 people in 2002). These are growing rapidly and include links to many foreign countries.

With advances in computer technology and email, an increasing number of people are now able to work from home and use the Internet to send their work into the office. This growing trend looks set to continue, with more than 200 Internet service providers in 2004.

 Did you know?

There are 77.8 million radios in Germany and 51.4 million TV sets.

 Did you know?

Over 89 per cent of people under the age of 14 have a mobile phone.

In Focus: Cars in East Germany

Before reunification, cars were not widely used in East Germany because the state wanted to encourage people to use public transport. Today, however, cars are used increasingly for journeys to work, shopping, holidays and recreation because they are relatively cheap to run, especially over short distances. However, the growing popularity of road transport, especially cars, has created problems in towns and cities. These include traffic jams, accidents, pollution and a decline in the use of some forms of public transport. Many cities have banned cars from their centres and created pedestrianized zones to improve the environment. Another problem with car transport is that groups such as the poor and single mothers, who may not have access to cars, are disadvantaged if the public transport system is not adequate for their needs.

CHAPTER 10

Education and Health

Most children start school in *Kindergarten* (nursery) at the age of three. Germany was the first country to introduce schooling for young children and this educational model has now spread to many countries of the world. Education is state funded and is compulsory for up to 12 or 13 years from the age of six. There are some religious and private schools, but most children are educated in the state system. Children attend primary school for four years from the age of six.

▲ Germany was one of the first countries to appreciate that play gives children a good start to their education.

SECONDARY EDUCATION

At the age of ten, children are divided into streams and allocated to a type of school. Some go to a *Realschule* (intermediate school), others go to the *Hauptschule* (secondary school), and others go to a *Gesamtschule* (comprehensive school). The most academic children go to the *Gymnasium* (grammar school). Each type of school offers general education and training, although the *Realschule* and *Hauptschule* concentrate on technical skills. The school day starts at 7.30 a.m. in summer and 8 a.m. in winter, and most children go home for lunch. There is a mid-morning break of about 30 minutes when children are free to play and to eat food they have brought from home. The day ends in the early afternoon, between 2 and 3 p.m.

UNIVERSITIES

At the age of 18 or 19, the more academic students take the university entrance examination called the *Abitur*. This is very rigorous and may involve six one-hour exam papers. All students must study at least one foreign language at school and at university; English and French are the most popular. Students study for a Diploma, or a State Examination or a Master of Arts or a Doctorate. Bachelor (BA) courses have also recently been introduced at many universities. The minimum period of study is $4\frac{1}{2}$ years, but it is usually nearer seven years. This, together with military service for men, means that most graduates are at least 28 years old before they start work. Slightly less than half of all students are women.

 Did you know?

Founded in 1386, Heidelberg was the first university in Germany. Since then it has grown in importance as a centre of knowledge and research in all areas of science, arts and medicine. It has 30,000 students from 80 nations in 18 faculties.

◀ Heidelberg University was founded in 1386 by Count Palatinate Ruprecht I. It now has a student population of 30,000.

COMPETITION FOR PLACES

Germany has 290 universities; they are mostly run by the local state and funded in part by the federal government. Parents are legally required to support their children's education and those who cannot afford to do so receive assistance from the federal government. There is a high demand for university places, which means that students have little choice where they will study. A central board allocates places and students may then swap places among themselves. This, however, is not possible in some subjects, such as medicine, where there is a high demand for places. German university students are keen to study subjects such as history, engineering, business studies and literature, but they are also interested in newer subjects, such as media studies.

Education and health

- Life expectancy at birth male: 75.2
- Life expectancy at birth female: 81.2
- Infant mortality rate per 1,000: 4
- Under five mortality rate per 1,000: 5
- Physicians per 1,000 people: 3.3
- Health expenditure as % of GDP: 10.8%
- Education expenditure as % of GDP: 4.5%
- Primary net enrolment: 87%
- Pupil-teacher ratio, primary: 14.8
- Adult literacy as % age 15+: 99

Source: United Nations Agencies and World Bank

Focus on: Vocational training

Vocational training combines on-the-job training with more formal classes. Germans regard qualifications (awards that are broader than just academic degrees) as very important and all school students are expected to work for some qualification. In this way, vocational training has the same prestige as more formal academic examinations. Specialist vocational schools called *Berufschulen* have been set up throughout the country to ensure that vocational training is of the highest quality. These schools specialize in training for a specific trade, such as carpentry or plumbing.

HEALTHCARE

Germany has an extensive and efficient health service, which is largely privately funded. All towns over a certain size have a hospital and most have emergency rooms to deal with accidents and emergencies. Ambulances are fast and efficient, even in rural areas. Citizens from other EU countries receive free first aid and emergency health cover, but there are charges for other forms of medicine. A network of local doctors dispenses most treatment and, apart from major operations, it is unusual for a patient to go to hospital for treatment except in an emergency. Instead people pay to go to a doctor in private practice. Doctors diagnose and give prescriptions (*Rezepte*) which have to be taken to one of the many chemists.

Germany has suffered from the spread of the HIV/AIDS virus. In 2004 there were 41,000 people living with this disease. Each year about 660 people die from AIDS-related illnesses, but new and improved treatments have been introduced with a greater number of specialist treatment departments in hospitals.

A network of dentists serves the local population in private practice. They carry out almost all the treatment themselves in their surgeries. Again, emergency treatment is free for people from EU countries, but there are charges for additional treatments.

ALTERNATIVE MEDICINE

Germans are very health conscious, and pharmacies offer a wide range of alternative or complementary medicines, including homeopathic medical cures. Special spas and hotels have developed to give people a choice of therapies such as mud baths, brine baths and detoxification regimes.

Diets are very popular in Germany, where some 20 per cent of people are classified as obese. This condition is particularly acute among young people and is the result of a diet often based on foods high in fats and salt and a lifestyle which is largely sedentary. People are being encouraged to take more exercise with the development in towns of keep-fit trails (*Trimm-dich-Pfade*) in parks and wooded areas.

▲ On World Aids Day, people in Berlin and other German cities light candles to remember those who have died from the disease.

OPPORTUNITIES FOR EXERCISE

In winter, skiing is a popular form of exercise for many people, especially cross-country skiing (*Langlauf*). Germans also like to play football and ride bicycles. There are special cycle trails in towns and across country areas to encourage more people to cycle to work.

In an effort to improve the health and wellbeing of the people, city planners have created green spaces in heavily built-up areas such as the Ruhr. In the 1990s, when coalmines closed in the Ruhr, the local planners took the opportunity to develop parks with wooded areas and keep-fit trails. In total, 27 million trees were planted in the Ruhr between 1980 and 1999.

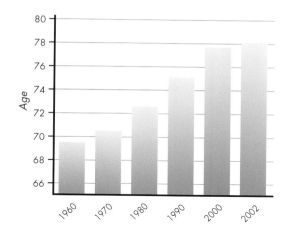

▲ Life expectancy at birth, 1960-2002

 Did you know?

Wheelchair users are generally well catered for in Germany with many lifts and ramps, but people with other disabilities, such as deafness and blindness, are less well provided for.

 Did you know?

The most frequent cause of death in Germany is from a heart attack; the next most frequent cause is cancer. These illnesses are largely the result of diets that are too rich in fats and salt, and of a lack of exercise.

▼ German cities, like Hamburg, below, have keep-fit trails so that people can take daily exercise. These trails are well used because many Germans are overweight and keen to recover their fitness.

CHAPTER 11

Culture and Religion

Germany has numerous festivals and celebrations, many of them dating back to pre-Christian and medieval times. In Munich there is the famous autumnal Oktoberfest, at which large quantities of beer and *Wurst* are consumed in celebration of a successful harvest. On Easter Sunday, children search their gardens for Easter eggs hidden by their parents. One of the most recently introduced celebrations takes place on 3 October each year; for this, Germans organize parades and funfairs to commemorate their country's reunification.

▼ On May Day in Bavaria, people wear traditional costumes and join in festivals of music and dancing.

A MUSICAL HERITAGE

Germany has a rich cultural history, especially in music. Johann Sebastian Bach (1685–1750) wrote famous concertos, cantatas and religious music, including settings of the Passion. At roughly the same time another German composer, Georg Friedrich Handel (1685–1759) wrote operas, instrumental works and church music, including the famous *Messiah*. Ludwig van Beethoven (1770–1827) composed many famous symphonies despite losing his hearing in 1819. Other important composers were Johannes Brahms (1833–97) and Robert Schumann (1810–1856), both of whom are famous for their romantic piano music.

PLAYWRIGHTS, NOVELISTS AND POETS

One of the most famous German writers is Johann Wolfgang von Goethe (1749–1832) who wrote poetry, plays and novels. His most famous play, *Faust*, tells the tale of a man who sells his soul to the devil in exchange for knowledge and power. Friedrich von Schiller (1759–1805) worked with Goethe and wrote plays such as *The Maid of Orleans* and *William Tell*. Other authors include Thomas Mann (1875–1955) who won the Nobel Prize for Literature in 1929. Mann's writings focused on the problem of the artist in bourgeois (middle-class) society and his works include *Dr Faustus* and the short story, *Death in Venice*.

Bertolt Brecht (1898–1956) wrote novels, plays and poetry and produced plays for the theatre. In the 1930s, his communist sympathies made him a target for the Nazis and he was forced into exile in the USA. He wrote scripts for films in Hollywood but left the USA for East Germany in 1947, where his communist beliefs found favour. Günter Grass (1927–) is a more recent author of plays, novels and poetry which take a sceptical look at modern society.

 Did you know?

Albert Einstein was a German physicist who developed the theory of relativity. He was awarded the Nobel Prize in 1921. He moved to the USA in 1933 and became an American citizen in 1940. In 1932 Werner Heisenberg became another Nobel Prize winner for his research on hydrogen.

Focus on: Marlene Dietrich

Marlene Dietrich was born Marie Magdalene von Losch in Berlin in 1901. She went to acting school, then worked in German silent films in the 1920s. In 1930 she became world famous as a seductive cabaret singer in the German film *Der Blaue Engel, (The Blue Angel)*, and was quickly signed to Paramount Studios in Hollywood. She moved to the USA where she became a major star. Her success was based on her beautiful, sophisticated, mysterious presence as an actress. In 1937 she took US citizenship and, a committed anti-Nazi, sang to the Allied troops during the Second World War. After 1945 she made a few well attended public appearances and took the leading role in a handful of carefully chosen films. She died in Paris at the age of 90.

▲ This statute of the writer and poet Goethe is in Berlin. It marks his major achievements as one of the first important German writers.

ARCHITECTURAL ACHIEVEMENTS

Germany has buildings in a wide range of architectural styles. These include the Gothic, that dates from 1200 when cathedrals such as Cologne and Magdeburg were built to dominate the surrounding area. From the seventeenth century, the Baroque period led to the construction of some giant castles, such as

▼ This futuristic building is the Sony Centre in Berlin, one of the many new offices and apartment blocks built since the reunification of the country.

Karlsruhe Castle, which also dominated their surroundings. In the eighteenth century, the strict geometry of the neoclassical style produced structures such as the Brandenburg Gate, which is based on a Greek design.

In the nineteenth century, longer spans of glass were used in buildings. This was the result of the introduction of steel, with its great supporting strength. The Art Nouveau movement used large areas of glass to create beautiful windows in department stores such as the Wertheim store in Berlin. The Bauhaus movement developed in the twentieth century and was led by Walter Gropius. Bauhaus stressed the functional nature of objects and buildings in their appearance. More recently, older buildings, such as the Museuminsel in Berlin are being restored, and new glass and steel constructions such as the Sony Centre are appearing on the skyline.

ARTISTS

In Germany, the impact of the Renaissance of the fifteenth century is best seen in the paintings of Albrecht Dürer (1471–1528). He produced many drawings of nature and animals in exact detail. Much of his work is still on display in museums in Munich. Later, Max Liebermann (1847–1945) was a forerunner of the impressionist school of painting in Germany.

 Did you know?

Aachen cathedral, Cologne cathedral and Speyer cathedral are UNESCO world heritage sites. This means that they are believed to be of sufficient beauty and architectural interest to be considered worthy of continued preservation.

DIFFERENT FAITHS

Christianity is the main religion in Germany and its two main branches, Protestantism and Catholicism, share roughly the same number of worshippers. The German constitution guarantees religious freedom to all. The division of the country into a largely Catholic south and a largely Protestant north dates back to the Peace of Augsburg (1555), which allowed the ruler of each state to choose whatever religion should be paramount within his or her state. Immigration has also affected the distribution of religions in the country. For example, the arrival of French Huguenots in the late seventeenth century gave a big boost to the Protestant population of Berlin.

In 2003, followers of Islam made up 4.4 per cent of the German population. Most members of the Islamic population are Turkish former guest workers who have now settled permanently in the country. The main Islamic centres are Dortmund, Dusseldorf, Frankfurt and Essen.

Before the Second World War, there were about 530,000 Jews living in Germany. The Holocaust and emigration devastated the Jewish community. However, Jewish emigrants from the former Soviet Union have swelled the numbers living in Germany in recent years. There are now about 11,000 Jews in Germany, more than 5,000 of whom have come from the former Soviet Union. The largest groups are in Berlin, Munich and Frankfurt-am-Main.

▲ This synagogue at Worms is the oldest in Europe and is a reminder of the importance of the Jewish faith in Germany.

 Did you know?

Germans who belong to a recognized denomination have to pay a church tax of 9 per cent of their income.

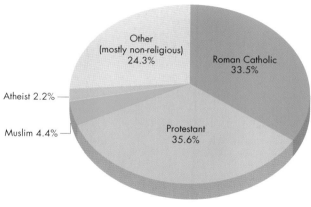

Roman Catholic 33.5%

Protestant 35.6%

Other (mostly non-religious) 24.3%

Atheist 2.2%

Muslim 4.4%

▲ Major religions

CHAPTER 12

Leisure and Tourism

▲ As people in Germany have become wealthier they have gained more leisure time and the means to enjoy sports such as sailing, as here in Hamburg.

Sport is an important part of German life. People enjoy taking part in or watching a range of sports, from football and cycling to sailing and skiing. In school, special classes above and beyond the normal physical education lessons help pupils develop their skills from an early age. There is a wide range of gyms and other facilities to encourage people to keep active later in life.

 Did you know?

The Bergen-Belsen memorial lies 60 km (35 miles) north-east of Hanover in the grounds of former Nazi prisoner of war (POW) and concentration camps. There are marked graves and monuments to remind people of the suffering and deaths that occurred here under the Nazi regime between 1940 and 1945. There is also a documentation centre that provides visitors with a history of the camp and its victims.

FOOTBALL

On a typical winter weekend, more than 300,000 people will be watching football matches throughout the country. The *Bundeslegia* (Football League) of Germany is important in Europe, and German teams take part in the Champions League of Europe every year. This is a competition between the top teams from each European football league.

In their leisure time Germans are very social and enjoy visits to their families as well as to the cinema and to cafes, where they consume rich pastries, cakes, coffee and herbal teas. Gardening is a popular pastime and Germany has many garden centres offering a wide range of plants.

SPA TOWNS

Tourism in Germany has ancient roots. The Romans had holiday resorts such as Aachen, where the rich could go to relax. In the eighteenth century, spa towns such as Baden Baden became popular. The water in these spas was believed to have medicinal qualities: drinking and bathing in it was thought to cure a range of illnesses. Wealthy Germans visited the spas for the healing waters.

In the nineteenth century, mountain climbing became popular and people from all over Europe converged on the peaks in the Alps, such as the Zugspitze (2,963 m/9,721 feet) in Bavaria. People also visited the mountains to enjoy the clean, clear air and the beautiful scenery. Sea bathing became popular in the nineteenth century. At first rich aristocrats, but later middle-class tourists, travelled to the Baltic coast to enjoy the sand and the sea. The increasing number of railway lines made it possible for many more people to travel all over Germany and Europe throughout the nineteenth and twentieth centuries.

▲ The spa at Baden Baden is famous for the healing qualities of its waters. People come here to bathe in the waters to ease muscular and arthritic pain.

Focus on: Berlin

Berlin is a site of great historical importance in Germany because of its postwar history. In 1961 the Berlin Wall was built, dividing communist East Germany from capitalist West Germany. The Wall was built across streets, and houses were demolished to make way for it. Families were split up, and sometimes did not see one another for many years. Checkpoint Charlie was a famous place where people were stopped to show their identification papers when crossing from one side of Berlin to the other.

HISTORIC TOWNS

More recently, cheap air travel has meant that more people can visit Germany's attractions. Cultural and historic towns such as Heidelberg, Cologne and Dresden attract many tourists, as does the picturesque valley of the River Rhine with its castles and gorges. In addition to the coastal resorts and spa towns, Germany has vibrant cities such as Berlin and Hamburg. Here the museums, bars and nightlife attract thousands of visitors. Some of these are people attending business conferences, and they make an increasingly important contribution to the cities' economy.

▼ Tourists visit the new glass dome at the Reichstag, which reopened in 1999 in Berlin. The dome provides a viewing gallery and represents Germany's commitment to 'transparency' in government.

Germans themselves are enthusiastic about travelling abroad. Many Germans visit the surrounding countries of Switzerland and Austria where people speak the same language and there are wonderful resources for winter sports and summer hiking. Millions of Germans also travel to enjoy the warmth and sunshine of the Mediterranean area. Countries such as Spain, Portugal, Turkey, Egypt and Tunisia are especially popular. Many Germans own second homes in some of these countries.

IMPACT OF TOURISM

The growth of tourism in Germany has created some environmental and social issues. For example, the influx of a large number of tourists can change the social structure of a small town. Once the visitors arrive, local

businesses become geared towards the tourist industry. At major tourist sites, such as Unter den Linden in Berlin or Garmisch-Partenkirchen in Bavaria, local people appear to have no other function than to act as guides or salespeople. In this way, the character of the town or village is altered.

In rural areas there are other issues arising from tourism. For example, the popularity of winter skiing in the Bavarian Alps has led to the creation of an increasing number of ski runs. This in turn has reduced the vegetation cover on the mountainsides and exposed the soil to erosion by wind and water.

However, there are many advantages arising from the growth of tourism in Germany. Tourism is a major industry and millions of Germans depend on it for their livelihood. New jobs have been created in hotels, restaurants and in nightclubs in Berlin and other large cities. Jobs have also been created outside the major cities, in villages and towns such as Rudesheim in the scenic Rhine Valley. People are employed driving taxis, acting as ski guides, and making and selling souvenirs.

▲ The Alps in Bavaria are one of the best areas for skiing in Germany. They are high enough to have snow and ice for more than four months of the year.

 Did you know?

Christmas fairs are very popular in Germany, and those in Munich, Berlin, Münster and Heidelberg are famous. They attract visitors from other European countries, as well as Germans doing their Christmas shopping.

Tourism in Germany

- Tourist arrivals, millions: 17.969
- Earnings from tourism in US$: 19,158,000,000
- Tourism as % foreign earnings: 3
- Tourist departures, millions: 73.3
- Expenditure on tourism in US$: 53,196,000,000

Source: World Bank

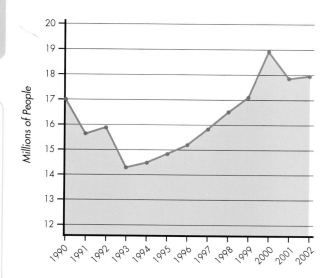

▲ Changes in international tourism, 1990-2001

CHAPTER 13

Environment and Conservation

The growth of Germany's towns, villages, industrial sector and population has put pressure on the country's environment. Relatively few places in the country have escaped the impact of people and their works. Land is still being lost to new roads, airports, factories and housing developments. Many river courses have been changed to permit the development of internal shipping routes. Many other watercourses have little life in them, showing the impact of past pollution from factories and cities. Air pollution drifts across from surrounding countries such as Poland and the Czech Republic, both of which had less strict environmental protection laws when they were controlled by communist governments.

▼ Despite years of legislation and progress in environmental pollution control, there are still problems of air pollution by factories, like this one near Berlin.

IMPROVING STANDARDS

Most Germans are aware of the importance of protecting their environment and much progress has been made in improving environmental standards. Catalytic converters are fitted to most German vehicles and, since 2001, there has been an EU requirement for the same anti-pollution technology to be fitted to all vehicles. Levels of some pollutants, such as carbon monoxide, have been halved as a result of the new measures. In an attempt to encourage more people to use public transport, the German government levies an ecological tax on petrol. The tax is used directly to fund public transport developments such as new or more regular bus services, or to develop integrated bus and train centres to make transfer between different modes of transport easier. Despite these efforts, there are still smog alerts in some cities during the summer.

Environmental and conservation data

- 📂 Forested area as % total land area: 15
- 📂 Protected area as % total land area: 31.7
- 📂 Number of protected areas: 7,607

SPECIES DIVERSITY

Category	Known species	Threatened species
Mammals	76	11
Breeding birds	247	5
Reptiles	16	n/a
Amphibians	20	n/a
Fish	95	6
Plants	2,682	12

Source: World Resources Institute

POLLUTION OF THE SEAS

In 1988, 18,000 dead seals were washed ashore on the North Sea coast of Germany. Scientific research established that the seals had died as a result of pollution of the seas by metals such as lead, zinc and mercury. These metals had weakened the immune systems of the seals and made them prone to a range of viruses.

Germany is one of the countries around the North Sea that has reduced pollution from metals and from fertilizers, pesticides and phosphates in an attempt to improve conditions for sea life, including seals. So far this process seems to be working and the sea is cleaner now than it has been at any time since the 1970s.

◀ Since the 1990s trams have again become an important means of public transport in German cities, such as here in Heidelberg. They provide quiet, fast and pollution-free travel.

In the 1970s and 1980s, Germany's rivers, especially the Rhine, were so badly polluted that stretches were declared a hazard to human health. This environmental disaster spurred the government into producing whole river plans designed to improve water quality in both the Rhine and the Elbe. These plans have greatly reduced the pollution of the country's rivers by farms, factories and cities. A measure of the success of these plans is the fact that, in 1997, salmon and sea trout were found in the Rhine for the first time in fifty years.

 Did you know?

The environmental group Greenpeace is very active in Germany. In the 1990s, Greenpeace protesters successfully prevented the oil company, Shell, from sinking an old oil platform in the North Sea.

RESTORING WATER MEADOWS

In 2000, a plan called 'High Water on the River Rhine' was set up. This aims to reduce flood damage by restoring former water meadows which used to help absorb the impact of flooding. It is hoped that the programme will be completed by the year 2020. The scheme takes the form of payments to farmers to encourage them not to plough up fields in flood plain areas but to leave them as traditional water meadows.

 Did you know?

The golden eagle has begun to breed again in some of the Alpine areas of Germany.

▼ Walkers in a German forest in 1998 are surrounded by evidence of acid rain damage to trees.

ACID RAIN

One environmental challenge that Germany is meeting is acid rain. All rain contains some acid because the water dissolves gases, such as sulphur dioxide, in the air. In the last twenty years, the rain has become more acidic because the amount of sulphur dioxide in the air has increased. Acid rain damages plants, especially trees where the new growth can be destroyed and the whole tree may die. Acid rain also kills fish and plants in lakes and rivers. In Germany, special filters are fitted to power stations to reduce acid rain. They filter out the sulphur and nitrogen gases. German industry is now using gas, rather than coal, to fire power stations, because it emits fewer dangerous gases. The German government introduced these measures in the 1980s and there has been some improvement in the water quality of lakes and rivers, but damage to trees from acid rain is still a problem.

IMPROVEMENTS IN WILDLIFE PROTECTION

Despite its problems, Germany has been successful in improving its environment. In the forests of Bavaria and in the east, wild boar, wolves, adders and deer are starting to increase in numbers. Similarly, in the Alpine areas chamois (a type of deer) and ibex (a type of goat) are multiplying rapidly. Other species such as the beaver, the horseshoe bat and the eagle owl, which in the 1980s were threatened with extinction, are now enjoying special protection.

Germany's national parks were created to protect and preserve wildlife, plants and areas of outstanding natural beauty. It was feared that the expansion of farms, mines and towns would threaten the existence of these areas. Today the environment in these parks is carefully controlled and monitored to ensure there are no developments that will damage or destroy

their natural attractions. Even in cities, areas of poorer housing are being redeveloped to improve the environment and air and water pollution are being reduced. The introduction of more areas of green space and forest means that the quality of urban life has been improved.

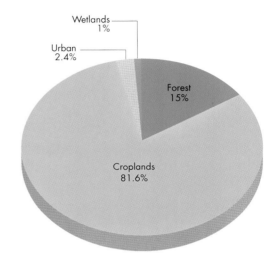

▲ Habitat type as percentage of total area

▲ The European wolf was hunted almost to extinction in Germany, but it is now making a comeback in some national parks.

CHAPTER 14

Future Challenges

Germany has changed much since its unification in 1871. It suffered division between 1945 and 1990 and then was reunified to its present size and shape. Despite all these dramatic changes Germany has become a rich, influential country, and the German people enjoy a high standard of living.

RE-INTEGRATION

However, there are still challenges for the future. Firstly, Germany must successfully complete the re-integration of the eastern areas with the rest of the country. Much progress has been made in terms of building new roads, railways and infrastructure. Eastern farms and villages have been modernized and factories have been rebuilt, re-equipped and reorganized. But much remains to be achieved in terms of reducing unemployment and rebuilding the infrastructure in the east.

Secondly, an ageing population and a declining workforce means there will be fewer people of working age to support the growing number of

▼ Young people like these, growing up in the eastern parts of Germany, are finding it easier to adapt to the changes than their parents and grandparents who grew up in a divided country.

older people. In future, Germany may need to permit more immigrants to enter the country to provide the necessary workforce. This could create problems because these new immigrants would not necessarily be able to gain German citizenship.

Thirdly, Germany needs to focus on environmental improvement in the future. Environmental awareness has increased in the last ten years and there has been progress with issues such as domestic recycling, the use of catalytic converters on vehicles, and the establishment of national parks and protected areas. Nevertheless, of the hundred or so mammals on the 'red list' (the list of endangered species) about one third are still in danger of dying out, including shrews and field mice.

A COMPETITIVE ECONOMY

Economically the country has not enjoyed the rapid growth of the 1960s and 1970s, mainly because of the costs of redeveloping the eastern regions. In future, an increasing amount of the country's wealth is likely to be derived from service industries, such as finance and tourism, and hi-tech industries, such as computer manufacture. The challenge here is to develop these industries in ways that enable them to compete successfully with other suppliers of global services and hi-tech products, such as the USA, Japan and China.

CENTRAL ROLE IN THE EU

Germany's economic and political power and influence within the expanded European Union will provide a good platform from which it can meet these various challenges. Within the EU, Germany continues to drive forward the move to a single European currency and is encouraging more members to join. Germany is

▲ An ageing population means that Germany may encounter healthcare and pensions problems in the future.

still developing its relationship with Russia and attempting to bring Russia and Europe closer together in economic and political terms. Globally, Germany sees itself as the 'conscience' of the EU. It opposed the invasion of Iraq in 2003 and is keen to help the EU develop a more ethical foreign policy. Germany continues to speak out about the need for a united approach to other important world issues, such as terrorism. It is also keen to extend its influence in the Far East, especially in China which it sees as the major force for change in that region.

Timeline

1st century BC Clashes between German tribes and the Romans.

768-814 BC Charlemagne rules most of Germany and unites the country.

1348-50 The Black Death kills one third of the German population.

1358 The Hanseatic League, a commercial association of German towns, is formed to trade between north and south Europe.

1517 Martin Luther starts the Reformation.

1618-1648 The Thirty Years' War ravages Germany.

1763 Prussia triumphs over Austria in the Seven Years' War and lays claim to part of Poland.

1806 Prussia is captured by Napoléon Bonaparte.

1815 Germany becomes a confederation of 35 states.

1871 Unification of Germany.

1914-18 First World War.

1920-30 Economic collapse and hyper-inflation in Germany.

1933 Adolf Hitler becomes Chancellor of Germany and the Nazi Party comes to power.

1939-45 Second World War, at the end of which Germany surrenders.

1946 Germany is divided into a communist East and a capitalist West.

1948 and 1950 East Germany confirms alliances with the Soviet Union.

1953 Revolt in East Germany is put down by troops.

1959 West Germany is a founding member of the European Economic Community (EEC), the forerunner of the European Union.

1960-70 West Germany economy grows strongly and consumer goods are cheap.

1970 A sharp rise in terrorism in West Germany, with the abduction and assassination of political figures.

1980-90 A steep increase in the cost of consumer goods in East Germany.

August 1989 Massive emigration from East to West Germany. Churches lead opposition to the communist regime.

9 November 1989 Berlin Wall is torn down.

August 1990 East and West Germany are reunified.

2000 Germany celebrates ten years of reunification.

2005 The European Union is enlarged to 25 members.

Glossary

Baroque A style of ornamental architecture and decoration, popular in Europe from the late sixteenth to the early eighteenth century.

Capital Accumulated or inherited wealth.

Capitalism An economic system in which the means of production, distribution and exchange are in private hands.

Celts A people whose first known territory was in central Europe in about 1200 BC. They later spread throughout most of Europe.

Cog railway A railway used in mountain areas where a central cog beneath the train is engaged to help it climb steep slopes.

Communism An economic system in which the means of production, distribution and exchange are in the hands of the state.

Communist A follower of communism.

Constitute To make up or compose.

Directive An instruction or order.

Federation The union of several states, generally for political or administrative reasons.

Franks Germanic peoples living in Europe between the third and tenth centuries AD.

Gross Domestic Product (GDP) Total value of goods and services produced within the borders of a country.

Gross National Income (GNI) Total value of a country's income from goods and services produced by its residents both within the country and elsewhere in the world.

Huns A wandering people that invaded the Roman Empire in the fifth century AD.

Industrial Revolution A series of economic changes based on the use of new machinery and steam power in factories. It started in the UK in the 1760s and spread to the rest of Europe and later much of the world.

Infrastructure The network of roads, railways, canals, water and electricity supplies necessary for the successful running of factories, offices, shops and houses.

Lombardy A region of northern Italy which includes Lake Como and the capital of which is Milan.

Papal state An area of central Italy in which the Pope was the ruler from 756 to 1870 AD.

Plenary Relating to assemblies or councils, a plenary session is one attended by all members.

Prussia A state in north Germany which became the centre for the unification of Germany in the nineteenth century.

Sand spit A tongue-shaped area of sand deposited by the sea a short distance off shore.

Silicon An element occurring in sand, quartz, granite, feldspar and clay, used in the manufacture of solar cells.

Soviet Union A huge communist state in Eastern Europe that existed between 1917 and 1990, but ended with the downfall of communism. Following this, the Soviet Union was divided up into separate independent nations.

Water meadow A meadow that stays fertile because it is flooded from time to time by a river or stream.

Further Information

BOOKS TO READ

Continents: Europe
D. Flint
(Hodder Wayland, 2005)

Germany
S. Gray
(Children's Press, 2003)

If I Lived in Germany
R. Knorr
(Longstreet Press, 2001)

The Middle Ages: A Watts Guide for Children
W. C. Jordan
(Franklin Watts, 2000)

Understanding the Holocaust
G. Feldman and T. Schmittroth (eds)
(U.X.L. 2003)

What Came From Germany?
David K. Look
(Children's Press, 2002)

World Holidays: A Watts Guide for Children
H. Moehn
(Franklin Watts, 2000)

USEFUL WEBSITES

www.destatis.de/e_home.htm
The site of the German federal statistical office.

www.statistik-portal.de/Statistik-Portal/en
The German federal statistical office and statistical offices of the *Länder* site, giving information about population, employment, elections, education, housing etc.

www.germanculture.com.ua/library/facts
A site on German culture today, with various articles and help with language and grammar.

www.bergenbelsen.de/en
The Bergen Belsen memorial site, with information and maps on the former Nazi POW/concentration camp.

http://motlc.wiesenthal.com/
The Museum of Tolerance Learning Centre – a comprehensive resource on the Holocaust and the Second World War.

www.un.org/esa/population
The United Nations site, specifically the Department of Economic and Social Affairs Population Division.

www.cia.gov/cia/publications/factbook/
The US Central Intelligence Agency site giving facts and figures on Germany.

Index

Page numbers in **bold** indicate pictures.

About the Author

David Flint is Head of Primary Teacher Education at the University of Worcester. He has written numerous children's reference books on a range of countries. He is also the consultant on a television series for children about the United Kingdom.